SHE BECAME ME

A Letter to My Younger Self

An Anthology Presented by

Lentina Rogers

Enhanced DNA

DEVELOP. NURTURE. ACHIEVE.
Publishing Division

She Became Me: A Letter to My Younger Self

Cover Created by MRDesigns: MarvinRhodes@gmail.com

Photo credits: Lauren Dickerson, Patricia Tate-Robertson, Pierre Pullins and Aaron Styles

ISBN-13: 978-1-7334198-8-8

DEDICATION

I would like to dedicate this book to God, for giving me the strength, the courage, the ability and the discernment to select all the right people for this project. Through these amazing women, we wish to bless someone with these messages from our heart – providing letters to our younger selves in order to show that we have overcome every challenge, problem and adversity that came in our lives.

As always, thanks to my Mom and my Dad for making the best decisions for me until "She Became Me" and "I Became Her" and now "She, Her and Me" are Happy!

Thanks to my family and friends for supporting my thoughts, ideas and vision until they came to life!

Presented by Lentina Rogers

INTRODUCTION

By Lentina Rogers

I have always been an obedient child; a team player, a supporter, a giver, someone who is compassionate, concerned, a helper, responsible, accountable, decisive, direct, logical, analytical and reasonable. But what I finally arrived at and what has brought me full circle to my life's purpose, is connecting to my spirituality and realization of a deep calling to fulfill my life assignments. You see, I constantly ran from great opportunities that would require deep personal self-actualization. Maslow described the top of his *Hierarchy of Needs* by remarking that: "a musician must make music, an artist must paint, a poet must write, if he is to be ultimately happy" (Maslow, 1943). In other words, self-actualization is based on full realization of one's creative, intellectual, and social potential through internal drive (versus for external rewards like money, status or power). It took years of what I perceived as failed and successful experiences and the presence of confidants, comrades and constituents, to gain the courage and knowledge to dismiss the fear-based barriers that were interfering with me becoming my holistic "self". Once that light came on and I recognized I was prepackaged with all the necessary skills, gifts and talents. I just needed to accept the role that was the design for me.

With that being said, in 2018 I created *Butterfly Effects, LLC* where I provide profound and precise avenues to enhance the physical, emotional and mental quality of life for the next generation along with encouragement, empowerment and elevation of women through workshops, authorship, mentorship and friendship.

My first book, *The Sun in My Eyes*, is a self-development, inspirational book describing the first steps to intentional transformation. I have learned to take the responsibility to say "no", staying true to myself, rejecting negativity in any form. protecting my energy which I refer to as my "magic". I've found that walking in my truth is not always following cultural, social systems or traditional customs that brings uncomfortable or stressful feelings into my cup. I adopted the slogan, *"I will fill my cup first, then when my cup runs over, you may sip from my saucer".* This is where my healthy boundaries start at the saucer. Because I am a naturally giving person, compassionate and thoughtful of others, this boundary protects and balances my self-care needs. My hope is to be an example for women to be true to themselves.

This anthology was birthed out of a spiritual awakening when the idea plummeted into my spirit to write a letter to my younger self. The women included in this anthology plummeted into my spirit with a complete blueprint to follow. When I walk in my purpose, things seem to come to me effortlessly. Sometimes I get false preceptors and I get an inclination to change courses, but this spiritual thing is solid and I have learned to adjust my antennas and stay connected to the source. It becomes a smooth transition to get back on course. It starts with the sorting of self, to exhilarate, vibrate and elevate self-love. I'm fully committed to using my spiritual gifts and being obedient to my spiritual purpose. My goal is to cultivate happiness and wholeness through physical, mental and emotional wellness. Until you manifest self-awareness and unmask your emotions. your energy will project the quality of character you deflect.

TABLE OF CONTENTS

LENTINA ROGERS

AUTHOR BIO

Lentina Rogers is the Founder and CEO of Butterfly Effects, LLC. Lentina is recognized as a youth mentor, family success – motivational and inspirational coach. She is passionate about encouraging people and helping them identify and appreciate the value of their uniqueness. Currently, Lentina is a health care provider practicing in

Indianapolis, Indiana. Her medical specialization is as a Behavioral Analyst.

In 2018, Lentina chaired the organization's first annual *"Flowers in The Attic – Planting Seeds for Blooming Ladies"* workshop for girls ages 13 – 18. Lentina's vision for the 2018 Flowers in the Attic event inspired by the organization's mission statement "We seek to provide services to a younger generation through educational workshops that teach basic life skills to create a sturdy foundation for a bright and optimistic future." Lentina used the platform to plant seeds – educating and motivating young ladies, helping them understand the significance of being self-sufficient, the importance of having high self-esteem and the role it plays in building healthy relationships. As CEO of the Butterfly Effects, she has created the opportunity to empower, share, and put into practice her mantra - *"If you can change one thing, then you are capable of changing everything"*.

Lentina's accolades include working as a philanthropist with 20 plus years of experience in human services. She is also an accomplished author.

CHAPTER 1

DESTINED TO BE ME

By Lentina Rogers

As I reflected on my younger self, I realized I was not fully present in distinctive moments. In fact, I was disconnected in some ways. The one thing I can attach my passion to is creativity. Between 10 and 13 years old, my brother and I would create characters and a story line about a family and the ups and downs of their lives. We kept this going for years, long before reality TV or blogs were created. Although I had a safe, secure and prosperous childhood, I was only passionate about drawing and being creative.

Then life happened and I moved away from what I was passionate about and started my blending process. I can't recall the emotions I felt during those other popular life occasions. They were just emotionless memories like birthday parties. I had a lot of birthday parties every year from age 10 until 50 years old. It's kind of like I was smiling and enjoying myself on the surface, but not deeply as I have come to live my life out loud and full of passion now. I was living but not alive in a passionate or enthusiastic way. In the last five years, I have just gotten to a place where I want to be in an intimate environment, all by myself for my birthdays. I want to do things that have significance and have a personal meaning, to perpetuate my happy place journey like meditation or self-reflection to strengthen my spirituality. In my early years, the episodes that stuck with me more vividly were moments of fear or disappointment. I have come to believe that I grew up feeling guilty about wanting to feel more and that I was undeserving about feeling excited or experiencing extreme joy in many single moments.

I felt I didn't want to be happier than anyone else, so I didn't give myself permission to explore happiness. Who was I to be extremely happy? When most people seemed happy with being mediocre about everything, that was good enough. I would say to my younger self,

"Girl, don't be afraid to embrace life. You will survive every episode of the detour of your dreams to study psychology - that dream was delayed not denied. You see you loved people and were a natural giver and servant for others. Your teen pregnancy took you on a journey of marriage at age 22, becoming a mother of 4 sons and divorced by 30.

You will appreciate your journey. You will realize that the pain, shame and judgment bestowed upon you from those experiences was part of the process. You see God set you up for your come up. You needed to be in a judgmental position to truly connect and understand some people are a victim of circumstances and some people are the circumstances.

You will come to appreciate that God has blessed you beyond measures with strong emotional wellness, cognitive mental health and a discernment compass. People will challenge you along the way. Stay true to your inter spirit, it is your calling you hear. Take that chance, even though it might embarrass you, scare you or simply excite the hell out of you. But just do it and remember to stop from time to time to recognize and inhale because it is a gift to truly be alive in that single moment. Stop and smell the roses, indulge in the moment, feel it all the way through, wallow in it, soak it up, enjoy it. Make an emotional attachment that will last a lifetime."

What I know now is without emotions, we are lifeless. Emotions are the greatest gift that God gave us, to allow us to experience life in 3D. You see, a tree is just a tree, and a leaf is just a leaf, both of which are living things. But until we are aligned with our ability to experience emotions in its entirety, we are just a leaf on a tree that is living and not alive.

I constantly dimmed my own light and did not want to stand out. Instead, I wanted to blend in to make everyone else feel comfortable. I did not know how to embrace all my skills, talents and God-given gifts. I wish I could have shown my younger self all the confidence she already had; it was dormant, just waiting to bust at the seams. She just needed to pull the trigger. If only there was someone to help her see how great she was and supported her through all the opportunities she let pass her by, she could've experienced those opportunities much earlier in life.

I would hug, rock and tell her,

"You better use every skill you have, even if it makes you uncomfortable. You see, staying comfortable was your greatest barrier. You had the skills and raw ability do more than most people; therefore, you didn't feel the need to push yourself any further. This was the fear of succeeding and maintaining success that caused you to

be stagnant, and you weren't doing enough to ignite or excite who God designed you to be. Therefore, maintaining your comfort zone became effortless and emotionless. If only I could have shared with you what I know now; that you worud never fail, you would have just learned how to improve the model — and girl, you always had the ability, strength and faith to prevail and land on your feet. Hell, you would do better than most people landing on your knees if only you knew then what I know now. But as you sailed through life blending in, you were destined for greatness no matter which path you took.

You see, to be great is simple: You must develop your heart, mind and soul to embrace your emotional experiences that drive your spirit to serve yourself first before you can enable someone else. You will come to appreciate all that you are and live a very intentional life, full of passion. You will find the key to happiness and enjoy every moment in 3D when you choose to explore the seeds that were planted in your spirit from your environment and examine if it is serving your purpose or restricting your progress. You are now in your cultivation season to pursue happiness. That's when joy will come every morning!"

SHE BECAME ME: A Letter to My Younger Self

KATRINA GARNER

AUTHOR BIO

Katrina Garner is a proud African American woman who is a believer of Christ Jesus and loves going to church every Sunday! Katrina was born in Indianapolis Indiana and has been in Indianapolis all her life. She was raised on the northeast side of town and went to school (from elementary to high school) in Franklin Township. Katina tried college right after high school but due to the lack of family support and becoming a mother at a young age, she decided that the best thing for her was to get a job to provide for her and her child. Katrina had an opportunity to go through a program called *The Indiana Plan* which landed her "not a job" but a career in the construction field. Katrina began her career as an Operating Engineer and has now been on her job for almost eighteen years.

Through the obstacles of life, Katrina was able to go to college and get her Associates degree in Criminal Justice. She then kept pushing and received her Bachelor of Science degree in Criminal Justice. But, she didn't stop there! She is currently working on her Master of Science degree in Psychology!

Katrina is a loving and caring mother of three beautiful children - one that is nineteen years old and is attending college, a daughter that is fifteen and a sophomore in high school and lastly another girl that is twelve years old and in the sixth grade. Katrina is a busy wife and her children keep her busy as a very active parent. She is very supportive of all the sports her children are involved in, including football, wrestling, golf, volleyball, softball and majorette dancing.

Katrina wears a multitude of hats in her life. She is also the owner of Allure Experience Décor and More LLC. where she specializes in planning and decorating for events. She is known for making anyone's dream become a reality on their special day or for any event. Katrina loves to spend time with her family – even if it's just coming together for Sunday dinner or a last-minute Saturday family game night.

Katina loves to travel the world and she is a firm believer of making time in her overwhelming live to take a vacation at least once a year to show her children that there is more to the world then just their hometown. Katrina loves making memories, through traveling rather than through material things.

Katrina also believes in giving back through community service and volunteers on monthly basis.

Lastly Katrina doesn't have much free time to herself but when she does, she loves to cruise the highway of 465 on her motorcycle; playing her music thinking about the next "Boss move" she can make to better herself, for not only for herself but for her family.

CHAPTER 2

REFLECTION IN THE MIRROR

By Katrina Garner

As I look in the mirror at the age of fifteen, you would have been hanging out with friends and walking to the candy store a few streets over, just carefree with absolutely no worries except wondering what you were going to wear to school the next day, who was going to be walking the halls, who was going to get in trouble for not making it to class on time, or how to get change out of the bottom of your mother's purse for snack at lunch because school lunch was horrible. Instead, you were making sure your work uniforms were clean, stressing out about walking ten or more blocks to work, and worrying about how you were going to get back home. On top of that, you had to worry about getting to school each morning and making sure you had a place to lay your head and get a meal.

As I look in the mirror at the age of eighteen, you were worrying about the next chapter in your life after basically being on your own for the past four years now, since you were a senior in high school and was supposed to start planning your career path, such as attending college and even taking up a trade. Instead, you were trying to catch up on your high school education. Because of the many absences, you lost your credits and had to attend night school and summer school in order to graduate on time. Plus, you still had to work and figure out how to take care of a little human being inside of you because you found out you were pregnant.

As I look in the mirror at the age of twenty-two, you were a single parent to one child, attending college, and working a low-paying job to make ends meet. Just when you thought things were getting better, you had another obstacle in your life: You were now pregnant with another child and barely making ends meet. So, you had to make some major changes: You had to quickly dropout of college and find a better paying job. You went from working two jobs to working one (that was equivalent to the two) with great pay.

Things started to come together for you financially. You worked that job until your second child was born. At that point, you were a single parent of two working long hours. And as your babies were growing up, you started to miss out on their upbringing because of the occupation that you chose. As the year went by, you started to fully balance parenthood and work life.

Now as I look at my young reflection in the mirror, I would tell her this: You are a strong, beautiful individual despite the obstacles you have faced. You have managed to make it through. Now, you have three beautiful children who are looking up to you at this point in life. Continue to teach them so they won't make some of the decisions you've made. Even though they were mistakes, they were also lessons learned.

PATRICIA MARIE TATE-ROBERTSON

AUTHOR BIO

Patricia Marie Tate-Robertson, is the founder and CEO of *Patricia Pearls Inc.* an organization designed with the girl in mind to shine like the precious pearl she is. June 2011, Patricia earned an Associate of Arts degree in Psychology from the University of Phoenix. Currently employed by Veterans Affairs Administration as a Medical Support Assistant since 2008.

Patricia has a fourteen-year-old son who raps, plays football and basketball, she also has eight stepchildren. Her hobbies include but not limited to dancing, shopping, and being an advocate for Patricia Pearls. To expand the outreach of *Patricia Pearls*, she opened *"Pearls New & Used Clothing Boutique"*.

Dedication

I dedicate my chapter to my son Jeremiah and *Patricia Pearls*, it is my desire that they will always know that although life comes with many uncertainties with patience, perseverance and God there will always be a light at the end of the tunnel, and the only thing that can stop you is you.

CHAPTER 3

BETTER DAYS

By Patricia Marie Tate-Robertson

I recall growing up living at the back door of Meikel Street Park. You could literally open the back door of our family home and step into the park where there were swings, slides, merry-go-rounds, and kids running around playing. Instead of me going outside to play with the other kids, oftentimes I would go upstairs and look out the window, longing and wishing I was like them.

My face hid behind a mask for many years. I was afraid that I wasn't good enough, cute enough or smart enough. I often referred to myself as an outcast. On my mom's side of the family, I didn't have other siblings who were joined by the same dad, and on my dad's side, I didn't have other siblings who were joined by the same mom. I wasn't treated differently on my mom's side of the family; however, I do recall one of my sisters getting mad at me and referring to me as a half-sister. I'll never forget the pain that I felt in my heart after hearing those words, not realizing that for years to come, "half" would take center stage in my life. Truly for many years to follow, that's how I approached everything, half way doing this, half way doing that. I never placed one hundred percent of my existence into anything that was beneficial to me, reason being is when I looked in the mirror, there was nothing whole about the reflection that was staring back at me — absolutely nothing.

My self-esteem was zapped to the max. Oftentimes, I would look at my sisters on both sides and try to figure out why I looked different. I would cry and ask God, "Why is my nose so flat?" "Why am I so dark?" and "Why can't I say some words correctly?" Yea that too, I was in speech classes until I was in the fourth grade. I have a brother named Jesse and just saying his name was pure hell. When my mom would be ready for Jesse and my other brother to come in the house from the park, she would say, "Go tell your brothers it's time to come in." I hated to call his name. I would be so embarrassed because I remember people laughing at me, which was another notch on my low self-esteem belt. I actually had so many notches that depleted my soul: I was chunky, dark, nappy-headed and so much more, to the point I started making new holes for the new roles that devoured my life.

There is only so much a child can bear. Often times, I would think to myself, "Doesn't my mother know I'm wounded?" "Shouldn't she know that I don't love myself?" "Doesn't she know how torn I am?" But then I remembered her having to endure much pain herself; she was one of the strongest ladies I've ever known. I wonder if my life would have been any different if I had told her how broken I was and how I feared everything that involved large crowds of people. I was often asked to go to a concert or a place where a lot of people would be, but I always declined out of fear that I wouldn't fit in, or people would stare at me. My second husband took me to my first concert at the age of forty-seven. It was at age forty-two that I started to truly regain some sense of value over my life. This chick has been through a lot, but God still reigns and grants me new mercies daily. I'm forever grateful.

Today at the age of fifty-four, I have successfully launched *Patricia Pearls Inc*, a non-profit organization for girls. Its purpose is to help girls discover their inner and outer beauty at a ripe age and equip them with the proper empowering tools needed for a healthy future. I do not want any girl to suffer the pain I did as a child.

I'm grateful that now I am able to look in the mirror and see a reflection of God within me. I embrace the girl I was and celebrate the woman I am now. I know that looking in the depths of my eyes in the past would reveal stories — actually full chapters — of pain, fear and denials; however, taking a look in the eye of the woman I am today reveals strength, courage, drive, ambition and wisdom, knowing that I am God's masterpiece, beautifully and diligently crafted. I accepted in my tender years that God was transforming me into all that I am now — greater later! I've heard God gives his hardest battles to the strongest soldiers. I'm humbled and blessed that God did not allow me to face the battles alone. There were many times I felt like throwing in the towel, but it was then that God carried me, lifted the heavy burdens and provided me with an added dose of strength. My wings began to flap again as I continued my journey soaring to new heights. I'm a living testimony that no matter what storms I've faced in life, the sun will shine again if I hold out. My past did not dictate my future. Better days are here.

SHE BECAME ME: A Letter to My Younger Self

ALVA BRONAUGH

AUTHOR BIO

Alva Bronaugh lives in the Nashville, Tennessee area. She is a published contributing author, entrepreneur, artist and designer.

She has been married for over 33 years to Maurice Bronaugh, has two adult children and one grand-daughter.

She is an advocate for mental health wellness. Her mission is to help remove the stigma associated with mental health issues. She was diagnosed with Bipolar II at the age of sixteen and her life-long journey of research and proactively managing this condition has allowed her to see the struggles of many. She has found success in actively overcoming her struggles and encourages other to be aware, accountable and to build strong support systems.

Her heart's passion is to spread the message of positivity, light and love for with these traits the world can be changed.

CHAPTER 4

HI LITTLE ONE

By Alva Bronaugh

Hi Little One,

I am you at the ripe young age of fifty-two. When I started to write this letter, I wrote about the experiences we went through because I thought it would make for good writing. I talked about our past, the pain, our greatest hurdles and what we have endured over the years. I wrote about the time that was snatched away from us because we are bipolar and how we struggled through the darkness well into our mid-forties undiagnosed. I also spoke of how our diagnosis allowed us to begin the process of operating with a clear mind, and we no longer felt the constant struggle of dealing with suicidal thoughts. Then I remembered the greatest action associated with the power of growth is letting go of the past and living in the present, where you allow the goddess in you to thrive.

We lived many years dwelling in the past, so much so, that we missed dreaming about our future, planning our future, and envisioning great things for ourselves. Instead, we

22

chose to be filled with hurt and unforgiveness. It was never an intentional choice; it was all we knew. Then one day, I made a choice to read a book called *One Day My Soul Just Opened Up: 40 Days and 40 Nights Toward Spiritual Strength and Personal Growth*, by Iylana Vanzant, and at the age of twenty-eight, our journey began. I have this saying when I talk to people about changing their lives: "If you want to change your life, read a book," especially the Bible. Learn who God is for yourself; you will be blessed beyond measure.

Little one, you must know that people are who they are before they hurt you. They too have been hurt, and hurt people hurt people. Find your ability to be aware of thy own presence and power. Choose not to be frozen by the pain and hurt you experience; instead, be forever mindful of who you really are and be proud of yourself! You are in love with God, great, powerful, creative, loving, kind, pure hearted, beautiful inside and out, funny, positive, full of spontaneity, generous, a great encourager and a true goddess of love and light.

I know you never knew who you were, and it does take you more years than most to find out who you are. But we learned a very important lesson from the man I married, and that lesson is this: There is no required age limit for accomplishments. What I also learned is that the many lessons we encounter are stages of developing the character traits you need to fulfill your destiny. Your timeline is *your* timeline.

Destiny is like a seed that has been planted, and this seed needs to be in a specific environment or it will not grow. It must be watered, pruned from time to time, and nurtured. I believe the most important part of this process is finding the goddess within you because your goddess is the part of you that holds your power, your faith, your confidence and your inner warrior. You will have to fight to keep your seed of destiny alive. Fend it of the naysayers who will try to speak death to your greatness. Your goddess warrior will take you from surviving to thriving. No matter how hard it may be, you will thrive, and with this, you will have a passion for others to thrive as well. This is key in life, to be of service to mankind.

I live in a world of such division. It is the year 2019, and people of color are having a war waged against them. Women are still fighting for equality. Our homeless population is growing, and so much more. There are mass shootings on the regular and nothing is being done to stop it. With all of this going on, you may think we feel hopeless; however, we do not. Instead, we believe in continuously growing regardless of what is going on in the world. I may not have much, but I do have some things that make the world a better place. We have a natural desire to be the light we want to see in the world. I smile and speak to EVERYONE! I came to the discovery that a person can be touched by a simple "Hello, how are you today?" I also really care about everyone's response, because the world is a cold place; but you and I, we've made a choice to warm it up.

I have had hundreds of conversations with people I do not know. I listen, respond, offer a positive view and intentionally make it a point to encourage them in order to help them remember that they are stronger and much worthier than they think. This is how God made us, so do not be ashamed when people question your happiness or kindness because those traits are intentional for us. They make us happy and give us joy.

We are so creative. You like to paint, sew, make jewelry, decorate, cook, and travel, and you look at life through rose color glasses, which is so awesome for us! We love life! It does not take money to be happy; money just makes things easier. You do have to learn that the wealth within you is your treasure and yes, we are trying to figure out what to do with those treasures, and still trying to figure out who we are, what we want and when it's all going to come together. Have hope because we always keep trying and that matters immensely!

You will have many choices to make in life, and if I could tell you one thing to prosper you, it would be this: Always put God first, and know he does not require you to be perfect. All he asks is that you have faith, trust the plans he has for you, plans to prosper you and not to harm you. This simple act prepares and opens a path that is parallel to none because God is just and faithful.

A vital part of our faith is to understand the difference between spirituality and religion. Spirituality can be defined as placing your desire into growing and experiencing a divine relationship with God by seeking God yourself but not through the structured regiments set forth by organized religion. Religion usually entails adhering to a specific belief system. You will choose to seek him on your own. Always keep your heart open to listen to the voice of God and know he is a very forgiving God. Please do not use our relationship with God as a weapon to judge others. Our relationship with God is just that — *our* relationship. We believe love should be extended to everyone. We choose not to be the judge of jury to those who have a faith different from ours, even those who choose not to believe. Love conquers all, along with peace and kindness. This is who we choose to be. Lastly, here are my instructions to you on how to live our most valued lessons:

Non-judgment: I once read a book that taught a lesson on non-judgment, and over the years, I have narrowed my definition down to this: I cannot judge others based on my personal beliefs or opinions.

How I came to this conclusion was by the definition of judgment found in the dictionary, which listed a few of the following: the process of forming an opinion or evaluation by discerning and comparing; an opinion or estimate so formed; a formal utterance of an authoritative opinion; an opinion so pronounced; and a formal decision given by a court.

One morning, I decided to put this newfound principle into practice. I had taken a vacation day and chose to spend it with my husband and children. (Yes, we are married and have children, but I will leave that wondrous journey for you to experience it all for yourself.) We decided to go to the movies. I told myself I could not have an opinion about anyone or anything, and I could not have any thought about another person. I thought it would be somewhat easy, but I found it was not. I walked into the movie theater and there were all these people floating around. I would normally have a thought about how they were acting, what they looked like, etc. However, I immediately caught myself and instructed myself not to form final thoughts or opinions. Then I walked past a woman who had on a beautiful sweater, and before I could even catch myself, I began to speak the words, "Your sweater is beautiful." At this very moment, I realized the very statement I made, (although it was kind and thoughtful), was a judgment. This one action put judgment into perspective for me. For the remainder of the day, I chose not to project my likes, dislikes, thoughts, opinions or my moral choices onto anyone. This was a lesson that taught me how to accept others the way they were and how to listen without forming opinions. It also brought me peace and allowed me to elude a plethora of conflict. Peace is important because it means, "absence of conflict". This lesson, little one, is one of the most powerful lessons you will learn.

Happiness is intentional: This lesson was passed on from your sister Delores. She told you about it, and you researched it and made it a motto of your life. It is quite simple: you will encounter problems, struggles, pain and hurtful situations in your life, and honestly it can happen daily, just like good things can happen daily. But through it all, you have the power to choose how you feel. You can feel happiness, joy, and encouragement, and be open to learning from your mistakes and/or the mistakes of others. Life continues and each time you will gain understanding, like all the other times before, or you can wallow in your hurt, pain, frustration, and negativity. It is really that simple. Happiness is intentional!

It takes true strength to be kind and friendly: As you grow up, you will experience unkindness from family, friends and strangers. We have always hated being picked on and hated to see others picked on. As a child and teenager, the only way we knew how to deal with such actions was by physically fighting others. But as time passed and we began to mature, we found the greatest tool was to be the change we wanted to see in the world. We began a journey of opening our hearts to loving mankind and extending kindness with our actions and words. We step out into the world every day, armed with love, mercy, kindness, forgiveness, and words of encouragement, never using our words to harm others intentionally and being friendly.

It is not an easy task because people find it hard to escape the hurt they have experienced, and in return, many choose to hurt others because they have been hurt.

They oftentimes do not trust a smile and good tidings because other humans have used their kindness as a disguise to gain trust and then hurt them. I too have been there, thus I understand. With an understanding of all the inner workings, we came to find myself delving deep to conjure all the strength we have within to overcome the hurt and the pain. We as one consciously chose to be kind and friendly and it does take strength to do this every day. With God in us, it makes it possible.

Shifting from survival mode to thriving mode: Little one, this is one of those lessons I wish you knew from the day you were born. When you are in survival mode, you can only think about how you got there and how you are going to get out. You do not have a mindset that allows you to dream, set goals, envision your goals and/or manifest your prosperity.

However, one day as I was reading my Bible, the Lord said, "Your tide has changed." I asked God what he meant. He told me I would no longer survive, that this was not how a goddess or the daughter of the Most High thinks. I was told my shift was now that of a thriving spirit.

Thrive means "to grow vigorously (flourish)"; "to gain in wealth or possessions (prosper)", "to progress toward or realize a goal despite of or because of circumstances". Wow! This was exciting to say the least. On this day, the shift in our spirit and mindset was life changing. So, I say to you, always be thriving, never surviving.

There are a few last instructions I give to you, and if you do not understand, seek understanding because we do our best living by seeking wisdom on our own and not depending on others to seek it for us.

1. Never stop growing and evolving.
2. Always believe in yourself.
3. Love is not perfect; however, for it to survive, you must continually work on perfecting it.
4. Many people will think you're weird; however, weird just means you're different than others.
5. Embrace your uniqueness; it is how God created you to be.
6. Self-love is the greatest love you can give yourself. Now flourish little one.

I love you!

Alva

CARMEN GREEN

AUTHOR BIO

Carmen Green is a strong, difficult, dedicated, faithful, honest and loyal person. Regardless of what she may face, she holds true to her values and her character.

She has over 15 years working with children. She put herself through nursing school. She gained experience working with the elderly, in hospice. She volunteered for better part of twenty years in the community and in the schools. She's a board member for Hamilton Southeastern (HSE) Sports, "Mudsock Sports".

In her spare time, she loves to read and study various miscellaneous subjects. She loves to inspire, motivate and encourage others to reach their God given potential. She likes to write poems and watch various TV shows. Reading to learn and constant growth in all areas of her life are important to her. For example, in the year 2018, she went to school to learn sign language.

She has been featured on the front page of the Milwaukee newspaper.. She is a devoted mother of two loving children, a son and a daughter.

She hopes to one day start a non-profit organization helping communities work towards change around the world.

Let's hear what others have to say about her!

I have known Carmen for over 2 years. In that time, I have seen her as a hardworking, trustworthy person who I respect and admire. She is dedicated to her family and friends. Carmen is a genuine person who will be honest and straight forward but also compassionate and caring. I am truly honored to know Carmen.

Dorothy C.

****

Carmen and I met the year 2017 of Sept, under some very hard circumstances. She's not always had the "best of luck, as some of us might put it". I've been able to form a good impression of her and, her resilience with what life throws her way. Her goals are to be not only a better person, but a person of peace. She's a servant. She always willing to help others in their times of needed. She has a big heart for helping the children whether it be on her route her every Sunday in the children ministry. I have heard her often talk about how she enjoys the little people! She is a fierce protector for her children and provider and, other's children too. She teaches her children how to be better people by being an example and, engaged mother! Carmen's lifelong goal is to finish her non-for profit to help other mother's. My hope is that she'll continue to purse finishing her studies so she can continue to help others.

Lanette D.

****

Carmen Green has been a volunteer in our Kid's Ministry for over 2 years, she has demonstrated a great sense of loyalty has always displayed a high degree of integrity, responsibility, and ambition. She is definitely a leader rather than a follower. In addition to her excellent scholastic accomplishments, she has proven her leadership ability by organizing and maintaining order during high capacity service times. She has a very strong moral standing and will stand up for anyone and anything that is right. She is also a most dependable team player; she devotes her time and skill to our team every week. She is eager to help in any way possible and will fill in wherever needed. Her good judgment and mature outlook ensure a logical and practical approach to her endeavors. When placed in difficult situations Carmen demonstrates tact and professionalism to ensure our families are seen and heard.

She is consistent and reliable. Carmen has proven that she would indeed be an asset to any organization, and I am happy to give her my wholehearted endorsement.

Monette N.

CHAPTER 5

TRANSFORMED

By Carmen Green

Dear Carmen, my sweet and precious gemstone,

How could I have ever known that you will still be standing tall and strong than ever before despite each struggle, trial and tribulation you've been through? Oh, the mighty goddess you have become. You're like an internal superwoman and an external Queen-goddess. Your internal superwoman powers are, and have always been, strength and perseverance. Your external Queen-goddess superpower has always been the smile you constantly keep on your face.

Flash back,

Carmen, I know you don't remember when you were just an embryo in your mother's belly, forming to take on the challenges that were present before you were even conceived. I know you can't remember and maybe it was best. Throughout the whole pregnancy, your mother smoked and drank, and when you were born, your mother and other family members would tell you that you were born ready to fight. And as you were coming into this world with jaundice in your eyes and bronchitis in your body, your fight began. I believe this is when you learned not only how to fight but also how you would succeed. I can only imagine that the fight and taste of success were pleasing to your taste buds. It would be something that you will continue to see and experience throughout your life.

Flash Back,

Carmen, I know you remember this! Your mother and father moved around so much you never stayed in one place long enough to remember most things. It was pointless to meet people and make friends because you just were just going to move soon after. Around eight years old, do you remember sitting on the floor with your sister in your mother's and father's trailer home with no living room furniture, eating bread balls and peanut butter and watching a show on an old, small TV?

Flash Back,

Oh, I know you remember this one. When your father went to jail, you, your mother, your older sister and younger sister went to a shelter. This white woman named Julie who wore glasses used to come to the shelter and take you and your sisters out. She only wanted to help your mother. But your mother didn't have enough strength to recognize it enough and wanted to help herself.
Oh, I know you remember when you were in foster care and your third foster care mother loved on you and encouraged you to change your ways that had developed from your past pain. You know she was only doing it to help you see the strength that you possessed, showing you what love looks like. I know you liked her better than the rest. You also got to see while in foster care how the

system really doesn't care about the precious little people who are in their care. The very system that was set up to help you positioned themselves to constantly cause you pain, blaming you for your parents' mistakes and treating you like it was your fault.

Flash Back,

Carmen, you still have the heart of true gold and real love, a love like no other. You've learned to take your past hustle and hurt and build a strong and courageous woman within yourself. Now that you have children, you're raising them with those same attributes. You are raising your daughter to be a very powerful, motivational, supportive, nurturing, young lady. You're raising your son to present himself as a support system and to be a reliable King to his Queens around him. And might I say, you've done a fantastic job so far. Carmen, as I look into your past, I see everything that caused you pain also brought you happiness.

Hurt= Happiness
Pain = Perseverance
Tears = Healing
Tragedy= Tenacity
Persistence = Patience
Empty = Equanimity
Sadness = Strength

Surviving & Thriving Caterpillar

Caterpillar, Caterpillar, I say unto you! Do you know how extraordinary you are? Do you see the beauty you possess? Do you see the abundance of knowledge you hold? Don't tell me you do not see the beauty that lives within you! You can't tell me you don't see the strength that you possess! The obstacles you've overcome! The mountains you've had to climb! The valleys you have had to fight through and the heels you have had to climb just to roll down! Caterpillar, Caterpillar, I know that it was hard to survive from birth. I see the challenges you have faced just to survive. The hurdles you've had to jump over just to leap even more. The constant battles day and night, sunup to sundown, and even throughout the night. The sun didn't protect you, and the moon couldn't hide you from your battles to face that have come to haunt you. I applaud you for your will to continue to stand, for your will to continue to stay in courage and stay in the fight and not give up. I know through these times, you felt like you just could die, but whenever you thought of death, it brought you even more life. Caterpillar, Caterpillar, now that you have survived being a caterpillar, take your rest in your cocoon, and do it weary less! Now is your time to rest at ease and with peace, for you are not dying but preparing for your new stage of life. Oh, caterpillar put down your weapons and stop fighting. Go with ease and rest peacefully under the moonlight. Oh, caterpillar, caterpillar! I beg you to stop fighting. It is safe for you to put your weapons down and send your guards away, for under the moonlight, the moon night is here to protect you. Caterpillar, hasten into your cocoon with no worries. They'll keep you safe! Now rest peacefully in your cocoon for the day will soon come where you will blossom and bloom!

Caterpillar, oh Caterpillar, my Caterpillar. Where is my Caterpillar? It's me, the Caterpillar replies, with very strong, big, bright wings, and as bright as a clear sky, brighter than the sun light, and boastful and proud of what I've become. Can you believe it's the most beautiful thing anyone could ever see? Your very strong, bright and colorful wings! A caterpillar that's no longer a caterpillar anymore. But a strong,

(C) - courageous,
(A) - analytical,
(R) - radiant,
(M) - meticulous,
(E) - empathic,
(N) - nurturing, yet bold, joyful, delightful, bright, purposeful, meaningful, knowledgeable, and most of all, lovable butterfly that you've become.

Once a thriving to surviving caterpillar is now a floriation butterfly. Brighter than the sun through today! And even brighter than the moon at night possessing strength from yesterday. Ready to live for your tomorrow. Butterfly, I hope you see that those abundance of trials and tribulations, not to mention the many struggles you've faced as a caterpillar, made you this strong, beautiful, and bright butterfly you are today!

As you can see, Carmen, you will succeed at whatever you put her mind to because it is your destiny.

SHE BECAME ME: A Letter to My Younger Self

PRECISS STONE

AUTHOR BIO

Preciss Stone, Experienced Registered Yoga Teacher (E-RYT), is the founder of The Yoga Lady LLC, A Mobile Yoga Studio based in Indianapolis, Indiana. The company motto is "Bringing Yoga to You" where the Yoga Lady brings the Yoga studio experience to the client or group.

Preciss is passionate about helping people heal themselves by way of yoga, meditation, stress management and healthy eating and she believes that each person individually possesses the power to heal themselves if they create the right conditions within their bodies. Her motto is, "You are your own healer".

Preciss, is an activist for race relations and inclusivity within the Yoga community and other fitness modalities. She is continuously educating herself by way of trainings, workshops, literature, and being in the field. For inquiries you can reach her at; TheYogaLady@hotmail.com or follow her @theyogalady317.

CHAPTER 6

QUEEN

By Preciss Stone

Dear Young Queen,

Life can be difficult to navigate, but you're going to make it! But first, you must go through a multitude of events along your journey. You will ultimately learn to fully love yourself in all your glory. That means the good, the bad and the ugly parts of yourself. You will understand why you reacted the way you did to different situations. Beautiful Queen, you are light, and you will learn that your spirituality, meditation, yoga and turning inward will tremendously help you as you navigate this life. You will learn healing is a lifelong process. You will be forced to dig to the core of your issues. Learning to love yourself unconditionally is the path to healing and working through past trauma.

Young Queen,

There is no replacement for the father figure you never had. It's not your fault your dad wasn't there for you. You will not find fatherly comfort in men, especially older, damaged, toxic men, for they need healing too. You are not at fault because your dad could not provide you with the love, guidance, support and nurturing you so desperately needed and craved. You will learn that older men cannot fill that fatherly void in your heart. Searching for that love in someone other than self will only lead to more anguish, hurt and pain.

Beautiful Young Queen,

It is ok to feel every emotion that you're feeling but be careful not to attach more toxicity to those emotions as you transition into healing your mind, body and soul. Such attachments will only lead to the well that will drill deeper into the pit of you.

Young Queen,

I will tell you that suppressing feelings will only lead to more emptiness and longing for more of the things, people and situations that don't serve you. You have to let it go. I will encourage you to seek wisdom from women who were in your shoes. You will learn to distinguish the difference between those who want to meddle in your business and gossip about you versus those who genuinely want to help you and have your best interest at heart. Trust your intuition; it will never steer you wrong. Most people of color are taught to keep everything bottled up inside. We tend to suffer in silence. Queen, you don't have to suffer in silence. Seek and find the help you need.

Nubian Queen,

You are worthy of pure, unconditional love, even if it's in

the form of self-love, which must come before you can truly allow anyone to fully love you. Continue to be patient with yourself as you sort through the pain of past trauma that is so deeply rooted within. Healing is not linear. You can heal and hurt from the same situation over and over again. There are layers upon layers to peel away and sort through. Remember, you are doing great!

Beautiful Queen,

You are not damaged goods. You are perfectly imperfect. Healing will take a lot of hard work. You are untangling old habits and thought processes in addition to rediscovering and finding yourself. You are evolving, creating new neuro paths in your brain, finding the wisdom and knowledge to remove yourself from toxic situations, and creating a healthier environment for yourself.

Queen,

Just know healing may become a lifelong journey and that's ok. Healing will require acknowledgement of past trauma. Face them head on, and sort through and learn from them so past patterns don't become repetitive. You are continuously growing into a woman of wisdom, not to keep it all to yourself but to help the next generation of traumatized young Queens who are suffering or suffered as you once did.

SHE BECAME ME: A Letter to My Younger Self

YALONDA BROWN

AUTHOR BIO

Yalonda J. Brown is on a mission to fully identify with her divine purpose by improving the lives of all she touches through her efforts. As an Author, Speaker, and Youth Experience Expert, Yalonda enjoys working with youth and women while being transparent about her journey and walk of faith to self-love and acceptance.

Yalonda is an avid reader and has always enjoyed all forms of writing since she was a young girl. As the CEO of Just Say It LLC, her goal is to create an impact though public speaking and published works. Mrs. Brown is a seasoned professional whose drive and self-determination has resulted in a myriad of accomplishments. Her expertise spans over twenty years in both private and public sectors.

"I love instilling confidence and speaking life into young people. As a parent and youth serving professional, I believe the trajectory of a young person's life is influenced by key exposure opportunities and experiences that build resilience and character." My faith, commitment and determination is a testament to overcoming self-doubt, disappointments and dysfunctional circumstances."

Yalonda enjoys traveling, shopping, and has a creative spirit. She is a lifelong resident of Indiana where she resides with her husband Vincent and a proud mother of daughter Kiara.

CHAPTER 7

"LISTEN, LONNIE, LISTEN"
By Yalonda Brown

Dear Yalonda (aka Lonnie):

I write this message to you as I reflect on the day when you were playing with a friend and you both were imagining the future. It was 1977, and you took a sheet of paper and listed every year from 1977 to 2010 in columns, and next to each year was your expected age. In times where *The Jetsons* cartoon was indicative of what the future would resemble, you had visions of what your apartment in space would look like. You imagined you would be married with children. Your career goal was to become a writer and a chemical engineer. In your mind, forty-two was the magic age of maturation and a life fulfilled.

Guess what? You lived past age forty-two. You are almost fifty-two, married to Vincent for five years, and the mother of a beautiful twenty-four year-old named Kiara. You are a published author and have enjoyed career success in both public and private sectors. You gave up on engineering pretty much after you spent multiple summers in engineering camps. You realized you were more creative,

48

and math and science were subjects you liked but did not love.

You can be quite stubborn and you will butt your head many times along your journey. At age nine, many of the lessons below will fall on deaf ears. Regardless, you will still live a fulfilling life (at least until you're fifty-one), and thank God for the lessons learned. Because you have always been a list maker, you tend to think and write in bullet points and you love acronyms. So, I have added some acronyms from the books you will publish.

- **L.O.Y.A.L.T.Y. (Loving on Yourself and Learning to Yield) is a way of life.** Don't waste your love on somebody who doesn't value it. You must learn to love yourself, so you know how to show love to others. How you feel about yourself will influence who you choose as friends. Being loyal to yourself means treating yourself with love and kindness, embracing what is good, and not just what you wish was different. Though you will experience heartbreaks and dysfunctional relationships, you are capable of loving authentically, forgiving yourself for when you fall short and forgiving others who will hurt you.

- **Care about the world around you.** Turn your passions into purpose. The world is much bigger than us and it doesn't revolve around us. Explore what you care about in the community around you. Be empathetic to the needs of others. Do not take the many privileges you will be afforded for granted.

- **Embrace your full lips and natural hair.** At this age, kids are cruel. They tease you about your full lips and pick on you because of your long beautiful hair. Guess what? There will be a time when full lips will become fashionable and highly sought after so much so that individuals even seek surgical means to have them. By this time, you are already getting your hair straightened with a pressing comb. I wish someone would have told me to never get my hair chemically relaxed. For the past eight years, you have not gotten a relaxer and you will love being a curly girl.

- **Being educated and speaking well is cool.** You were reading the newspaper at age 5. You have grown up with an appreciation for education and the development of a vast vocabulary. You are often teased as "talking white." Your ability to write and speak well will open doors for you in a variety of settings in and out of the workplace. Don't get it twisted, you will become street smart as well. There is even a socially accepted term called 'code switching' where switching from African American vernacular to a 'white voice' is a skill to communicate in diverse settings and with all types of people you will encounter.

- **Have elephant-sized vision.** You are a big thinker. You are not afraid of taking risks. You are victorious, not a victim. Failure is an option. You will grow through it. Live boldly with no regrets but consider the consequences of your actions. We are warriors, not worriers. You will make mistakes.

Please know that your mistakes do not define you. Be awesomely you. You are enough!

- **Keep your financial house in order.** Money isn't everything, but not being a good steward of your finances will cause you much anguish and pain. You will develop a dysfunctional relationship with money, and it will take you years of struggling and credit recovery to get back on track and reach a comfortable level of financial stability.

- **Be B.R.O.K.E.N.** God has placed in you everything you need in order to do the things you were placed on earth to do. Faith develops perseverance. Through the many trials you will experience, know that God loves you unconditionally. Being B.R.O.K.E.N. stands for Breaking and Removing Obstacles with Knowledge of God's word, Evidence of His power and Never ceasing prayer. By now, you have already begun your walk with God as you have accepted Christ and been baptized. Though you will fall short many times in your Christian walk, God will show you time and time again that He stands on His promises and His grace is sufficient.

There is so much more I want to say to you. You were blessed with two praying grandmothers who loved you dearly. They have both passed on, but their legacy lives on in you. So, as they would often cover you in prayer, I end with a "Prayer for Lonnie":

Prayer for Lonnie

Lord, when Lonnie has a sense of purpose, I pray she will not lose it. Give her the wisdom and motivation to take the right steps every day.

Enable her to understand what is most important in life, so she can make decisions and choices easily.

I pray she will never fail to consider her destiny in every choice she makes and in everything she does.

Help her not to have her mind made up without consulting You. Keep her from insisting on what she wants instead of wanting what You want. Instill in Lonnie a desire to always be in the center of Your will.

In Jesus Name,

Amen

SHE BECAME ME: A Letter to My Younger Self

RONIEKA HOWELL

AUTHOR BIO

God's Girl :: Sacred Woman :: Creative Spirit :: Encourager :: Motivational Speaker :: Author :: Wellness Practitioner :: Organic Mixologist :: Business Consultant :: Digital Marketer :: Web Designer :: Prison Ministry Advocate :: Foodie :: Kitchen Queen :: Tea Lover :: Urban AG Farmer :: World Traveler :: Music Lover :: Abstract Artist ::

Ronieka is a mother, daughter, sister, friend, entrepreneur, mentor, and international social ministry leader. Born and raised in Indianapolis, Indiana, she discovered her purpose early on which was to live an abundant life, work smart, and to treat others how she wanted to be treated.

Over the years, Ronieka has continued on her mission to love, encourage, motivate, connect, and to build women up who have been broken. She has always found joy in uniting, inspiring, giving back, and helping women heal through their hurts, push through their pain, and W.I.N. again through her personal/spiritual development workshops.

CHAPTER 8

MY PEACE, MY PURPOSE
By Ronieka Howell

Dear 16-Year-Old Me,

You probably just stumbled across this letter because it has been stuck in one of the many journals of your unfinished lists of bright ideas, projects, business ventures, and things that you want to do in life, that's buried deep down in the box of keepsakes that you've been collecting all of your life, with hopes to someday share them with your own children. I am writing to you from the future, a passing of time and chain of life-changing events that have taken place, yet offers a great deal of knowledge, personal growth, and enlightenment on our life.

By now I'm 27 years older than you are, and I'm sure you are still a know-it-all, and probably don't want to hear what I have to say. But I'd like to share some wisdom I've learned along the way. First, get up, brush your teeth, and get in that tub and marinate! You know Momma don't play about our hygiene! Put on some clothes and look like you are going somewhere, even if you have nowhere to go! I know you have better things to do like go meet that drug-dealing boy from the projects that you're not supposed to be around. He's no good for you, but what do I know? The future surely holds a different perspective and a different taste for men that I wish you could see! I'm praying that I might be able to help you grow, find your purpose, make peace with the family secrets, forgive those who wronged you, and learn to walk boldly in the anointing that you probably haven't realized you have yet. Will you please put your stubbornness to the side and listen to what I have to say?

I see you're trying to fit every personal item in that milk crate that you are packing up, so that you can leave with that boy. You're planning on moving out because you're mad at Momma for cussing you out for coming home late after curfew. You thought she'd be drunk again when you came home. But she was sober, waiting on the front porch with rollers in her head, smoking on a cigarette, as you slowly came prancing across the dark park. She had words for you that you weren't expecting, but it was words that you'd prayed for because you were in such a rush to be grown and to move out on your own by all means necessary.

Pump your brakes sis, life is not as bad as you would have everyone think it is. Plus, you're only 16 years old. What do you know about life? It's a jungle out there in those streets, and you will have to lie, steal, cheat, and do degrading things with your body that you don't even want to imagine, just to survive. The only comfort that you will get will come from you spilling out your heart through your writings in your journal, because the moments you'll encounter will be too embarrassing to share with a human being, so they will be suppressed deep inside your womb.

One thing that you should know is that your breakthrough will come through your relationship with God! He is going to be with you every step of your journey. The more you acknowledge His presence and talk to Him, the more He will guide you! You are going to have to trust Him in the wilderness and dark situations that will seem like you are never going to make it out of. You will cry your heart out, but giving up will not be an option, for it will only delay God's plan for your life.

You feel alone right now, like you don't fit in, and you are trying to understand the things you see that no one else can, the feelings you feel that warn you to go a different way, or even the love that you have for people who wrong you the most. My prayers are with you and my heart is heavy because I too know what it feels like to be used, abused and expected to smile and look pretty. In spite of it all, you are smart, beautiful, creative, gifted, and filled with a purpose that only you can fulfill. Let's fast forward to 2020!

After years of learning through trials and errors of living life, you graduate high school, go to college, and become licensed to do so many things. You become a business owner, a virtuous wife, a loving mother, and a loyal friend. You help birth ministries, pour into women with shattered hearts, and experience hurt from those closest to you. You encounter a brokenness that you thought you wouldn't live through. You face challenging health issues, and smoothly transition from that 13-year unfaithful marriage, into a season of singleness that leads to your sacred self-discovery and an abundant new life.

You made it through it all baby girl, by finally facing the wall that held you captive. You were awakened and used every gift that God placed inside of you to create. You succeeded, you regained your confidence, and you saw the blessing in everything that you ever lost. You now operate on a frequency that requires those around you to rise up.

Always remember to trust the process, self-evaluate, and stay focused. Life is full of decisions we make that ultimately shape the end result. Take care of you first, love others, and do what makes you happy. Find your peace within. Encourage others, be kind, and be the best version of you that you can possibly be. Be unapologetically you! Believe in yourself, invest in yourself, and continue to heal yourself. Be patient. Remember that you are a light in darkness, a powerful force, and you can do all things through Christ who strengthens you!

Love, Your Older Self,
Ronieka LaShann

JANIE SUE FLYNN

AUTHOR BIO

Janie Sue Flynn was born to a 15-year old mother in eastern Kentucky which was coal miners country. She grew up in Chicago, endured a turbulent childhood as a result of the relationship between her and her step-father. She ran away from home and repeated the generational history of her mother and had her first child after marrying at 15 years old. By the time she was 17, she had two additional children. As a result of her unstable childhood, she made a lot of bad choices, endured a lot of pain, dropped out of high school and married into an abusive relationship. BUT GOD! With the love and help of some good Christian mentors, she accepted Christ into her life and learned the importance of forgiveness.

After her children started school, Janie Sue finished high school and two years of college and enjoyed a successful career in network marketing and sales.

Today, Janie Sue is a proud mother, grandmother of five and great grandmother of ten! They have always been her blessings and the very best part of who she was and is today. She lives in Indianapolis, Indiana and works part time with special needs children. Janie Sue is happily married and shares her life with her best friend and soulmate.

Janie Sue realizes that she has been through a lot of hurts and hurdles. She is hoping that by sharing her story, she will help someone else realize that they are a survivor. Two quotes that Janie Sue lives by are: "Life is short – only listen to the positive things and don't let the devil whisper anything negative into your ears" and, "Women are like tea bags. You never know how strong they are until they are put into hot water".

CHAPTER 9

DEAR YOUNGER SELF....

By Janie Sue Flynn

It has been a while since I asked you to come out of your safe place where I have kept you tucked away for such a long time. Your younger years were challenging and painful; you were so young and innocent. You never got to experience what it was like to live a normal kid's life.

You have always been strong, although no one ever told you that. Adults failed you as a child; always using negative words by telling you that you were "stupid" or "you looked slouchy". You were told that you were not wanted and would never amount to anything in life.

Younger me, those things really hurt your spirit, didn't they? What doesn't kill you makes you stronger in life, little one. If I could give you some advice, dearest younger me, I would tell you to learn to take all that negative and use it as a motivator. Let your drive be positive and achieve your goals in spite of them. Never expect someone else's opinion of you to become your self-worth.

Your life was good until the family moved to Chicago and mom remarried. Your stepfather was a monster and tried to destroy you. But.... he didn't know how much of a fighter you were. Even then you just didn't know your own strength. He sexually abused you and tried to diminish your spirit. Again he didn't know how much of a fighter you were. He hated that about you so much.

As you grew older into a teenager you held onto a lot of anger in your mis-spent years. You remember Joe? He was also older and was your first interaction with boys. He was 18 years old just graduated and you were 13. You trusted him. He treated you very well. His mother treated you as if you were her own daughter. You spent a lot of time with Joe and his mother. That was a place where you felt safe and warm, it was a comfort you never felt in such a long time. It felt really good to feel that type of love again. But it didn't last very long.

The family moved to Bremerton, Washington and you hated it. You felt really isolated and alone. Eventually you made a friend across the street and things got even worse. Your friend had secrets too. One night you spent the night at her house, and her own father molested her even while you were laying right beside her. You decided to lie still and in silence fearing that he would molest you too. You were so thankful that he left you alone. You reached over and hugged her while tears were running down her face. As you wiped her tears away, you asked her how long this had been going on and she responded since she was 8 years old. You told her this had been happening to you too; since you were 6 years old. You both hugged each other in silence until you both fell asleep.

This made you very afraid of men. It made you not trust; it made you feel like you had to run away. Running away was a way that you handled any uncomfortable situation. You were so scared you didn't know what to do, so you decided to call your friend, Joe and told him about the sexual abuse of both you and your friend. Joe was so angry, he mailed you money to come back to Chicago. The next day you came home and your stepfather had found the letter with the money in it. He intimidated you and threatened to send you to an all-girls school. You had suffered enough, you couldn't stand it anymore. Again, you ran. Running for you happened throughout the majority of your life.

You then went to live with your grandparents for a while. It was always a loving and peaceful place. You felt settled there until, even your grandpa betrayed your trust and touched you inappropriately. You never would have thought that your own grandpa would abuse his granddaughter. It took time, but you eventually forgave him.

But, as always you ran...

You found your father in Indianapolis, Indiana. You hadn't seen him since birth but you did know that you had six other brothers and sisters and that brought you joy. After living with your father for a while, this also ended badly due to him drinking too much. He would beat you for no reason. Life continued into one consecutive misfortune after another.

At your dad's house, you met a man who eventually became your husband.. You had two beautiful daughters together. He was also an alcoholic like your father and was both physically and mentally abusive. They say you follow a pattern and you did. After several years of abuse, you ran again.

Those next six years were difficult for you, trying to raise two children alone. But for the first time, at 26 years old, you started to realize who you were and who you were not. Some independence felt good. You didn't need to feel like you needed a man. A friend fixed you up on a date with a family friend. You dated for about four years, then you married him. Your life was finally "normal" and your children felt settled. He was also a very good father. Only, there was one thing missing in your relationship. There was not a lot of affection. Your children felt settled and happy and that is what was important at the time. You often felt lonely and the old feelings and insecurities crept out. You fell into a deep depression, gaining weight, and you couldn't understand why because your life was the most settled it had ever been. For the first time you really wanted to fix yourself. You were tired of running.

You sought therapy, and when you went, it went well. You learned so much about yourself and life in general. You were grateful to the therapist for help and support. You also turned to God and surrendered your life to Him. Life became better.

Younger me….. I am taking you out of your hiding place and holding you close. I'm filling your little heart with all the love and affection you have always deserved. I would tell you that sometimes life can be hard for all of us. I would tell you to get acquainted with God, and make friends with him. He will always be your true and best friend. You can always depend on Him, He is the key to your inner strength. He will always listen and soothe your soul, without faith we have no guide or direction. Have faith in something or you will fail in everything.

- Love yourself. If you don't love yourself first, no one else will!

- Stay positive in your thoughts, what you get back in life is what you put in it!

- Set goals in life. Spiritually, mentally, physically, and financially. If you set goals, you are more likely to achieve them!

- Stay away from negative people. They are poison to your soul!

- Most of all, be proud of who you are!

- Be your best friend!

- Take time for yourself!

- Reward yourself!

- Live life to the fullest!

- Janie Sue Flynn

SHE BECAME ME: A Letter to My Younger Self

LA TOSHA WALKER

AUTHOR BIO

La Tosha Walker is an Indiana native and the owner of Star Advocates Inc., a program that came about to help parents with children in schools that have or need an IEP to ensure the child's needs are being met daily for them to be successful in the classrooms and to ensure that the parent knows their rights and options. La Tosha is also the owner and Lead Photographer of Tsassy Photos. Since La Tosha was a child, she has taken photographs of everyday moments and small events in her life. La Tosha is a former freelance writer and photographer for the Indiana Herald Newspaper where she would cover a lot of the entertainment and current event news. La Tosha is a mother of four children - twin boys, Tyrell and Tyrese and two girls Mercedes and Ashleigh and enjoys spending time with her children and family.

La Tosha, also loves to volunteer in her community and help others. With a strong background in Early Childhood, La Tosha, has worked in Childcare with over 20 years of experience. The love for what she does made her want to become a foster parent to help mold the youth in the system and to let them know that anything is possible, but first you have to believe in yourself and never give up.

CHAPTER 10

FULL CIRCLE

By La Tosha Walker

As I think back on a younger me when I was placed in a peer counseling class in high school, it made me think about where it all started. There were about ten of us in the class, and it seemed as if everyone would pick me to talk with them about whatever problems they were dealing with, even though I never wanted to be in the class. Besides, I could really care less about what anyone was going through at that time anyway.

Looking back from then to now, I see it was a gift that I was trying so hard to escape from. I never wanted to be in anyone's business, and most of the time, I felt like I was walking around with a big Tell-Me sign across my forehead. And without basic needs, I would try my best to listen to the children and my peers who were going through so much and take action. Sometimes, the children who would confide in me were complete strangers, but I listened and gave them the same energy as if I had known them for years.

Fast forward to today, I feel like I'm still that rock people lean on and tell their problems to. I don't cut anyone off, and I always give my honest opinion even if it hurts a few people along the way. Thinking back, that class taught me a few things about loyalty, understanding, and perspective, and this has made me appreciate everything I have; even the toxic stuff I encountered as a child didn't draw me in. I can remember being told it was not always about me as a kid, and now I see that looking out for others would bless me in so many ways. I have always been the one to help others and now I see that the more you give, the more you will receive. Others gain such a great deal of respect for you that you're able to give so much and not ask for anything in return.

The countless hours turned into so many friendships and bigger opportunities while being a volunteer for different events. Friendship would be on my list, too. I grew up with one brother who is 15 years older than I am, so I depended on my friends like they were my brothers and sisters. I've never been afraid to ask or tell them anything, even if it meant that they would be mad at me. I think everything happened for a reason, and in time, my friends have stood with me through all of the different issues we've come across along this journey in life. I'd like to think of them as shining stars to my sky and everyone shines in a different way, but their light has been around to help guide me on my way with them. I learned from their failures and successes, and we are still growing into our destiny.

So, 25 years later, it has all come full circle for me as I had the opportunity to adopt two lovely little ladies. That is when I learned that you don't have to be blood to still want to protect and fight for whatever was in their best interest. Shortly after, I gave birth to a set of twins and now had a family that would completely depend on me. I realized that anything and everything I did would not only affect me, but it would have a ripple effect on my family, which was my biggest investment. So, with all the practice, patience, and understanding I learned from sitting in rooms with complete strangers, it helped me understand that it was never about me. It was about what I could do to uplift others.

-   *La Tosha Walker*

SHE BECAME ME: A Letter to My Younger Self

JASMINE GAMBLE

AUTHOR BIO

Jasmine is a 26 year old young and passionate youth advocate. She is dedicated to the clients she serves and their well-being well beyond offering services. Jasmine currently serves the youth in her community in numerous ways. She is a youth mentor, home base caseworker, and a competitive cheerleading/tumbling coach. Jasmine enjoys helping our young people reach their highest potential through mentoring and coaching. Jasmine's drive to work with our youth comes from her own personal experience with youth mentors and cheer coaches as a child.

Jasmine credits a lot of her accomplishments to the adult role models in her life. They helped her reach her highest potential, they believed in her, and helped shape her into the women she is today. Through all of life challenges, Jasmine often reflects on this quote "God wouldn't put me here to fight this war if he didn't create me for it".

Her journey to self-love is one with many twist and turns, but it is one that she has learned to embrace. Jasmine prides herself on helping our youth create, accept, and embrace their own individualized journeys in this thing called life!

CHAPTER 11

WE GROW THOUGH WHAT WE GO THROUGH

By Jasmine Gamble

Dear Princess Jasmine,

I wish I was there when you were younger to show you all the life lessons I've learned after growing up to prevent all the hurt you went through. I wish you knew how much you were loved and protected. I wish you knew that you didn't have to be scared to speak your mind. I wish you knew the word "no" and that it's okay to put yourself first. I wish I could have taught you how to love yourself before trying to love someone else because that would have saved you from all the hurt you have endured. You were a great friend, a great sister, a great protector of your siblings, and loved your family to the ends of the earth. But, if you would have shown yourself the same grace you showed others, you wouldn't have felt so low at times. If you knew your worth, self-love would have come so easy for you. Despite all the things I couldn't teach you when you were younger, you still learned those life lessons one way or another and you have blossomed into an amazing young woman.

Who would have thought that the relationship you have with God would ever be as strong as it is now? Your love and faith in Him has helped you come a long way. I am glad that you now know that you are never alone and that God is always with you. My mind is at ease knowing that you are a fighter and won't allow anyone to beat you down anymore. I am proud to know that you have finally experienced self-love and will always put yourself first. I know that sometimes boundaries are still an issue for you, but let's not downplay the fact that you have been able to tell people "no" and create healthy boundaries to protect yourself.

You are a great leader and mentor who is very independent and hardworking. The thing I love the most about you is your resiliency. If you think about it, you developed this trait at a young age because without resiliency you wouldn't have made it through the traumatic things you went through. You realized that not only does your little sister look up to you, all the girls you coach look up to you as well. Because of the love you have for yourself and others around you, you have no choice but to continue becoming a better you.

You are amazing and don't you ever forget it. ☐

TREVA SHULER

AUTHOR BIO

Treva Shuler is from Maysville, Kentucky and is one of three siblings from her mother Elizabeth (Libby), and one of six from her father, the late Paul King.

She is a very passionate person when it comes to her three amazing and talented kids. As a child she was raised to be a strong lady, independent and family-oriented and this carried over into her adulthood.

Treva searched for happiness in many ways, trying to prove

herself to others. As a mother at an early age, Treva felt she needed to prove that she could be successful - in her career and as a mother. After having her third child, she then turned to the church and started testing her faith.

Now, Treva is passionate about her career, but more importantly is focused on raising her children. In 2019, she married her best friend of 18 years. She is not only a wife and mother but is also a business partner with her husband in a general contracting company. In addition, for the past 10 years, she has served as a Property Manager for a non-profit Senior Housing Community in Indianapolis, Indiana.

Now that Treva has finally realized the value of self-care, she is happier than ever before.

CHAPTER 12

A LITTLE GIRL'S PURPOSE

By Treva Shuler

As I look into the eyes of my daughters, I can't help but reflect and utter these words of love, joy, pain, and encouragement to my younger self:

"Treva, I hug you because I love you as my child.
I kiss and tease you because I always want to see that beautiful smile.
I know you were told you wouldn't become anything as a woman, and
I know it hurts to hear someone say hurtful things about you.
I know it also hurts to be a fatherless daughter and not receive the love
a present father should show."

I was told I wouldn't be anything but a dropout with a lot of kids by a drug dealer. But my advice to you is to allow the negative things to motivate you to become the great woman, mother, sister and daughter you will be. Use that pain and hurt inside to also push you to become a better person on the outside. I know you started writing poems to get through your hurt and feelings of loneliness, but just know you are never alone.

And your face shows you are worrying on the inside. Ask yourself, "Who am I?" and "Why am I still here?" You have a reason to be here. You are a beautiful young lady who is loved by so many people. There are some adults who don't know how to show it or just don't make the time because they are working. But you are and will be a great person who will no longer need a shield to protect yourself.

Open your mouth and tell them about your pain so someone will know the pain you're feeling. Let them help! You're only a little girl, and I know that you've been touched. Believe me, others have seen the signs. I am here to protect you! Remove that shield from around you. He will never touch you again. You will be able to look him in his eyes and say, "I remember what you did to me." No more pain, no more fear. I am finally here to show you the strong woman you have become. I am not alone. I learned not to ask myself, "Why?" Instead, you will continue to shine into the better little girl.

You will use all the fire in your eyes and the pain in your heart to spread your arms as if they were wings — to fly into being a positive mother of three kids and a wife to a true man you can call your husband, who will help you continue your better life and show you what real love is. Look at what God has sent you. He has stood by your side through some of the hurt, pain and distrust in your life. You're over here smiling, and all that hurt doesn't control you any longer. Now show your kids how to walk through life and protect them. Give them what you feel you didn't have. Keep talking to your kids through me.

Treva Shuler

SHE BECAME ME: A Letter to My Younger Self

LATEENA PETTIS

AUTHOR BIO

Lateena Pettis was born on January 6, 1980, in Muncie, Indiana. Growing up, she enjoyed competitive sports, playing the violin, and hanging with childhood friends. However, during her childhood, she experienced much abandonment, abuse, and rejection. The insecurities that came along with rejection and abandonment did not allow for her to have healthy social relationships with children her age. She was always labeled weird, crazy or bullied for not being able to fit in. She managed to make a few friends, but there was still some doubt and insecurity in the relationships. During Lateena's teenage years, she was sexually molested. Lateena spent most of her high school years in depression, confusion, and suffering from PTSD from the abuse. After graduating from high school and never undergoing any therapy, she spent her 20s living through trauma and adversity because of the circumstances and crisis that she experienced during her childhood.

During her 30s, she turned her life entirely to Jesus after being in and out of church since a child. God began to save and heal her from her psychological bondage. She spent almost seven years working through PTSD, recognizing her triggers and perceptions with the help of prayer, therapy, and fasting. At the age of 36, Lateena begin to live life for the first time! She enrolled back in school and started to identify with who and why God created her and begin to live out her vision, purpose, and destiny. Presently she works with children who have severe emotional/ mental behaviors that are rooted in trauma.

She is a specialist in behavior strategies and de-escalation in crises. Lateena is currently in her third year in her bachelor's program, Psychology of Human Relations. Lateena plans to continue into a master's program to become a licensed therapist in the state of Indiana. Her vision is to remain focused on the foundation of family, specializing in restoration, communication, reunification, parenting, women empowerment, and childhood behaviors rooted in trauma. Lateena published her first book in 2018 titled, *Wait Don't Throw in the Towel,* a book to encourage biblically based marriage and reconciliation. Lateena also founded Perazim Empowerment, a multifaceted ministry that focuses on community, women empowerment, and worship.

CHAPTER 13

THERE IS A HOPE AND A FUTURE

By Lateena Pettis

"For I know the thoughts that I think toward you, says the
Lord, thoughts of peace and not of evil, to give you a future
and a hope."
— Jeremiah 29:11

Dear Lateena,

I know what you are experiencing right now, and I want to provide you with confidence. I want you to understand what the endgame is. You have a future and something to look forward to. Little girl, you are not forgotten, but you have been misunderstood by many. Time will be needed for healing and recovery from your trauma and adversity that was created by incest. This letter to you is my sincerest apology for not being able to help or support you during a vulnerable time in your life. Your thoughts are fully understood, and your fragile emotions will one day be stabilized. It can be very shaming to discuss being molested, especially when you're at an age where society deems "you should know better" or "you should have told someone."

Your story is not shaming, and you will overcome and break through the mental and emotional bondage that incest, rape, abandonment, and rejection have caused you. If you are wondering if you can tell someone without judgment that your own father raped you night after night until you became pregnant, you can tell me, and I will help you with your breakthrough. He took advantage of you, and it is okay to talk about your feelings, emotions, and mental state surrounded by the incident. You can discuss how foul his breath was and how he would talk dirty to you while he engaged in sexual pleasure. Trust me, little sister, you will overcome and break through. There is hope and a future for you. Do not allow anyone to make you feel like you wanted the sex from your father, although during the time of the abuse, your body craved the orgasmic feelings and needed the sexual gratification. It can feel shameful to feel like you wanted sex from your own father. But it was not you that wanted the sex; it was your flesh. Sexual feelings were made to feel good naturally, and it doesn't matter if you were raped, molested, or violated. Your flesh will enjoy it while your mind and emotions are in turmoil.

Child, you could not have processed that you were being raped multiple times because you were in survival mode. Hell, you had not lived with your own mother in over a year, and your grandparents did not know what to do with you. You needed help, love, support, and understanding, and while your grandparents did all they could, it was not enough for your breakthrough, healing, or deliverance. You were traveling to the destination that God had ordained for you, a hope to bring you a good future and to prosper you.

Being a victim has now just become a part of your identity and a part of your life. For a while, you will desire this negativity, and you will not know how to function without it because it has now become a part of who you are. But there is hope for you, to prosper you and to give you a future. Do not feel guilty or shameful; child, you were 15 years old. People are going to condemn, question, and blame you, but you will rise above all of that. During your healing, people, especially family, will not be able to help because they do not understand. You are going to have to forgive them and keep it moving. Don't wallow in self-pity and self-condemnation., and don't wait for them to accept you and give you hope. If you do, you will just be digging a hole for yourself because they will all misunderstand you. It is part of the plan to your healing, to isolate you so that your hope and future is solely in the hands of God and that no one can take credit for the miracles, blessings, and favor that will be bestowed upon you by God — because girl, there is a hope for you, a plan to prosper you.

Over the years, as you grow into a young woman, you will learn a lot about your true identity and who you are as you start to forgive and heal yourself and the ones who have hurt you. The road to recovery will not be at all easy, but it will be worth it. So, this letter is to let you know that I know the face of trauma and adversity you are wearing. But instead of leaving you ashamed, unworthy, embarrassed, and afraid, I want you to know who you really are.

Lateena Marie, you are first and foremost a child of the Highest God, a daughter of a King, and a co-heir of the kingdom of God through Jesus. You are beautiful, bold, and confident, and was called to walk in power and authority on this earth. You are destined for great things, and your salvation, healing, and deliverance will be a testament for many other young girls to receive empowerment, salvation, encouragement, and break-through from their tribulations too. You are not a hot mess, crazy, or mentally ill. You are resilient and peculiar. You are the light in dark places and life to dead things. When you go places, you shift atmospheres with what you have in you. You amaze people with your strength, passion, and commitment to serve and help assist others in crisis situations. You are a virtuous woman who walks with an unquenchable fire ignited by God. One day you will give your children all the love, fairness, and equipping that you did not get. You will see that there is more to life than hurt, pain, abandonment, and rejection. There will be true love and happiness with a man who loves you as he loves God and himself. It may take some years and lots of healing and deliverance, but you will overcome it. You will conquer the fear of your children being mentally ill and having social or emotional issues because of your own bondage. You will become a generational curse breaker. Your childhood trauma will give your own children a hope for the future.

As your life is given over to God to be saved, you will begin to walk in a new freedom and experience a new life. You will talk different, look different, think different, and slowly become entirely new. Yes, a child, a modern woman, a woman with hope, a future, and a completely different view of life. You will prosper! Get excited about the future, and allow the past to continue to push you forward in your destiny! You are the best woman I know, so get excited about the journey.

Love,

The Woman You One Day Will Become

Presented by Lentina Rogers

SKYE BERGER

AUTHOR BIO

Skye Berger is an Executive Leadership & Lifestyle Coach and the Chief Encouragement Officer at Door Opener Academy. Skye's professional background includes child welfare, mental health, addictions, facilitation, and program development.

Skye is a sought after expert in empowering youth and families while renewing the youth workers and organizations that serve them. Skye has reached international audiences through keynote, online and live facilitation experiences. Unparalleled in her desire and aptitude to engage her audience, Skye is able to cultivate excitement and synergy within individuals, families, and organizations.

This Gary, Indiana native holds a Bachelor of Arts in both psychology and sociology from Purdue University and a Master of Science in management science with a concentration in executive coaching and organizational behavior from the University of Texas. As a Six Sigma Green and Black Belt, Skye has applied quality management skills by focusing not only on policy and processes but connecting our workforces heads and hearts.

Skye is the mother of three young ladies and twin boys. When she is not paying tuition for her daughters at Indiana University and Purdue University, she tries to find her way to a beach. Skye resides in Central Indiana, with a heart for all things uplifting, creative and youth work related.

CHAPTER 14

REASON, SEASON OR A LIFETIME

By Skye Berger

Do you remember the poem, "Reason, Season, or a Lifetime"? I don't remember the first time we heard it, but its words always resonated with me to the core. I don't believe that every time you encountered someone, it was your intention to place them in one category or another. Recently we have considered, just maybe if we took this precaution, our interactions would be more substantial.

Our life has been colorful. The list of experiences is ever growing with exposure that has caused a milieu of opportunities.

This path has not been absent of adventure. At this point, it is my understanding that true reflection is a process, a heuristic journey to say the least, and never a destination. All of your interpretations have been challenged with new understanding through shared perspectives evolving your overall experience.

Our experiences have been many, and I want you to know that I still see you and your journey have not been in vain. I am stepping back to tell you what you never heard. I am reaching all the way in so you can feel the embrace. I am standing in the midst of your every word, your every thought, your every dream, and it is everything you could ever imagine based on the circumstances of your time.

The way you held onto your dreams is the evidence I am now living. We are truly living in the fantasy you created. Skye, if you have to choose one thing going forward, I encourage you to follow your feelings. Just follow where your heart leads. You are absolutely right about every thought you have about yourself. I remember the words that were spewed upon us like an explosion of all the resistance presented as barriers to your future dreams. I don't want you to listen to anybody who said your heart is selfish. I don't want you to listen to anybody telling you that your heart is up to no good. I don't want you to listen to anybody who could consider your heart to be cold. Let no word hinder your light and dismiss all that would not boost your shine. I want you to always remember that your heart is *your* heart. You are the only one who is accountable to the decisions that you make. Other people will be affected by your actions, which is why it is imperative that you move forward with the guidance of your inner most true self. Your heart is love. Your actions are love. I want you to hear that you are accountable to your feelings. So follow them.

We heard the opinions, we released the negativity, but we powered through by holding onto knowing that our true inner being is continuing to produce.

All the work that you're doing right now is a result of what you have experienced. Skye, it was hard but the necessity of your experience is going to benefit the children. The abuse, the emotional turmoil, your teen pregnancy — every bit of every drop of pain has been transformed into an international movement! We count it all joy because you finally realized the power within you.

You are currently second-guessing because outside influences are challenging your thoughts and deflecting you from the current path. Everything you're doing is exactly what needs to be done — don't change a thing.

Skye, your feelings are a compass. They will always lead you to the appropriate path. Stay on it. I cannot wait to see your manifestations!

CONTRIBUTING AUTHORS

AUTHOR CONTACT INFORMATION

Lentina Rogers	tinamac1966@yahoo.com
Katrina Garner	Mckinneyk398@gamil.com
Treva Shuler	trevaldavis@yahoo.com
La Tosha Walker	tsassyone@yahoo.com
Carmen Green	Zamarias.castle@gmail.com
Janie Sue Flynn	Janiesueflynn@yahoo.com
Alva Bronaugh	Alva.bronaugh@yahoo.com
Yalonda Brown	Justsayitllc2@gmail.com
Skye Berger	skye@skyeberger.com
Jasmine Gamble	Jasminegamble71@gmail.com
Preciss Stone	theyogalady@hotmail.com
Patricia Tate-Robertson	Patriciapearls1@gmail.com
Ronieka Howell	roniekalashann@gmail.com
Lateena Pettis	perazimempowerment@gmail.com

SHE BECAME ME: A Letter to My Younger Self

DEVELOP. NURTURE. ACHIEVE.
Publishing Division

www.EnhancedDNAPublishing.com
Denola M. Burton, CEO and Founder
DenolaBurton@EnhancedDNA1.com

Made in the USA
Monee, IL
27 May 2020